THERE IS HOPE! A Journey Through Seizures, Epilepsy and Brain Surgery
Copyright © 2011 by Carla Huelsmann

ISBN 978-0-9797999-8-3

Published by:
Waymaker Publishers
P.O. Box 1481
Fenton, MO 63026
email: info@waymakerpublishers.com
website: www.waymakerpublishers.com

All scripture quoted is taken from BibleGateway.com using the NASB translation except where specifically noted other translations are used.

THE HOLY BIBLE, NEW INTERNATIONAL VERSION®, NIV® Copyright © 1973, 1978, 1984, 2011 by Biblica, Inc.™ Used by permission. All rights reserved worldwide.

"Scripture taken from the NEW AMERICAN STANDARD BIBLE®, Copyright © 1960,1962,1963,1968,1971,1972,1973,1975,1977,1995 by The Lockman Foundation. Used by permission."

"Scripture taken from the New King James Version. Copyright © 1982 by Thomas Nelson, Inc. Used by permission. All rights reserved."

Contents may not be reproduced in whole or part without the written permission of the author. Contact author directly for permission to use or quote material.

Author's Contact Information found in back of book.

Printed in The United States of America. All rights reserved under International Copyright Law.

THERE IS HOPE

A JOURNEY THROUGH SEIZURES, EPILEPSY AND BRAIN SURGERY

CARLA HUELSMANN

About The Author

Living with epilepsy and seizures has been a life-long experience for me. At the age of two, I was diagnosed with epilepsy, a result of meningitis and being in two comas. At age 27, following the birth of my daughter, I struggled to keep the six to twelve daily seizures and/or auras (warning signs and feelings before a seizure) at bay.

For six years, many medical doctors and one alternative doctor tried new and old medicines to help me find the levels my body needed to control the daily seizures. Throughout the first 35 years of my life, these debilitating episodes began with a starry, day-dreamy, nauseated feeling followed by loss of speech, train of thought, confusion, and eventually sleep. After being misdiagnosed, I took a proactive approach and researched as much as I could about epilepsy.

Seizures, fears, and instability had taken over my life and affected the well-being of my family. Desperate to find some relief and some normalcy, my daughter and I prayed that God would provide answers. October 16, 2000, my prayers were answered when a doctor at the Mayo Clinic in Rochester, Minnesota recommended the necessary treatment. After two weeks of extensive testing and hospital observation in the Epilepsy Evaluation Center, it was determined that I was a good candidate for brain surgery. On November 7, 2000, the area of my brain that caused the seizures was successfully removed.

Recovery was difficult and frightening. I suffered from pseudo auras, panic attacks, fear, and post-operative depression. During this time, I received a book from a friend called *God's Creative Power of Healing* by Charles Capps. In the book, I found much-needed faith, hope, and inspiration.

Recovery included extensive therapy with a clinical psychologist. It has now been over nine years since my surgery. I have overcome fake seizures, fears, anxiety, obsessive thoughts, and depression. Six years without a seizure marked a miraculous milestone for me and my family.

Overcoming a challenging recovery and finding inspiration in the process has provided me with immeasurable life lessons. Through this book, I strive to help others avoid the same stumbling blocks that I encountered and to enjoy life to the fullest. This book glorifies Jesus Christ and teaches biblical principals. There Is Hope is an inspirational and faith building book for readers of both genders.

TABLE OF CONTENTS

About The Author		7
Dedication		13
Acknowledgements		15
Epilepsy Surgery Enabled Me To Live Life My Way		17
Let's Begin The Journey Together		21
1	My First Six Months	22
2	First Response	24
3	Keeping the Faith	26
4	Grade School Years	28
5	Pressure Cooker	30
6	What Others Think	32
7	Why Me?	34
8	Cutting The Caffeine	36
9	Alcohol And Drugs Don't Mix	38
10	Insecurities	40
11	Medications- The Good, The Bad	42
12	Searching For A Miracle	44
13	One Day At A Time	46
14	Major Medical Setbacks	48
15	Emotionally And Mentally Unfit	50
16	Another Seizure	52
17	What If I Have A Seizure?	54
18	My Pain Is Their Pain	56
19	Danger On The Road	58
20	Life Disrupted	60

Table of Contents Continued

21	My Four-Legged Friend	62
22	There Is Hope!	64
23	Miracles Happen	66
24	Epilepsy Evaluation Center	68
25	Medical History Journal	72
26	Tests, Tests, Tests	74
27	Auras	76
28	The Big Day	78
29	Brain Surgery	80
30	Intensive Care Unit Recovery	82
31	First Morning After Surgery	84
32	48 Hours After Surgery	86
33	Will I Stay Or Will I Go?	88
34	Going Home	90
35	Home Sweet Home	92
36	Psychogenic Seizures	94
37	Three Month Check-Up	96
38	Anxiety Attacks	98
39	Living Life To The Fullest	100
40	Is This Normal Jerking?	102
41	Six Months After Surgery	104
42	One Year Check-Up	106
43	Decreasing Medicines After Surgery	108
44	Three Year Check-Up	110
45	Finding Rest	114
46	Elevator Going Down — Emotions - Ground Floor	116
47	Doubt	118
48	Obsessing	120
49	Depression	122
50	Fight or Flight	124
51	FEAR False Evidence Appearing Real	126
52	Balance	128

Table of Contents Continued

53	Four Years After Surgery	130
54	Five Year Anniversary And Pursuing Dreams	132
55	Five Years Seizure or Anxiety?	134
56	Perfectly Fine	136
57	Annual Check-Ups	138
58	Six Year Set-Back	140
59	Medicine Free	144
60	First Reoccurring Seizure After Surgery	146
61	Conflicting Symptoms	148
62	Restarting Medicines	150
63	What If I Have A Seizure?	152
64	Adapting And Living With Epilepsy	154
65	Adjusting To Changes	158
66	Denial	160
67	Rejection	162
68	Acceptance	164
69	Moving Ahead	166
70	Victory Lane	168
71	Living Life To The Fullest	170
72	Pursuing Dreams	172
73	Inner Growth	174
74	Setting The Stage	176
75	Unburdening Baggage	178
76	From The Living Hope	180
77	From Me To You	181

Resources For Neurological Disorders — 182

AUTHOR'S CONTACT INFORMATION — 183

Dedication

This book is dedicated first of all to my daughter Kelsey who gave me the reason to live and survive the battles that were endured. She has been my blessing from day one and the encouragement I needed from start to finish.

Love you Kelsey,

Mom

Mom and Dad — For the tough times and the good times. You stuck by me and I don't ever remember a time in my life when you let me down. You two are awesome!

Love you from the bottom of my heart,

Carla

For all the readers who will read this book may you find much hope, help, and healing in your lives.

Respectfully yours,

Carla

Acknowledgements

Wisetown Baptist Church
R.R. 4 Box 70
Greenville, IL 62246

September 22, 2009

Dear Carla,

Thank you for asking me to write a letter for your book. It has been my pleasure to be your pharmacist for almost 25, years. I also count it a privilege to have been able to give you some spiritual direction along the way. As your family pharmacist and as the pastor of Wisetown Baptist Church, I had a dual opportunity to help you and to minister to your spiritual needs and concerns.

I had first hand knowledge of your medical condition and I observed the frustration and fear you went through as you struggled to deal with this disease and to find the right combination of medications to treat it. We had many conversations about your condition and how God would see you through. As you turned to Him and He opened the door for this wonderful surgical procedure, you knew there was hope.

I have read your manuscript and have found it informative, touching, and rewarding. It is my prayer that this personal account of your illness, depression, despair and victory will be a valuable help to others who experience this same hurdle.

God bless you as you continue to serve the Lord faithfully and praise Him for His goodness.

Yours in Christ,

Tom Rankin P.D.

Epilepsy Surgery Enabled Me To Live Life My Way

The following is Carla's testimony as posted on the web site for the Mayo Clinic:

Carla Huelsmann was diagnosed with epilepsy when she was two years old. As she grew, she learned how to manage her disease and the seizures that came with it. But as a young adult, her seizures began to grow worse and threatened to take over her daily activities; she realized it was time to find a new approach. That's when Carla turned to the Mayo Clinic. The help she received not only gave her relief from seizures; it gave her a new outlook.

"I have the confidence and capabilities to pursue goals that I had always dreamed about," she says, "but never thought possible, until now."

MANAGING THE DISEASE

Throughout Carla's childhood and into her early adult years, she experienced mainly petite mal seizures - seizures that involved a brief, sudden lapse of conscious activity. The seizures would cause her to stare off into space, a state she describes as "daydream-like". Occasionally, she experienced slurred speech and would lose her train of thought.

Carla recalls that having epilepsy made her school years challenging. "I was self-conscious about having seizures at school or in public. I did not want others to see me as being different."

Although she disliked having the disease, medication helped her keep seizures to a minimum. After high school, she attended college and got married. She had to constantly deal with her epilepsy, but the condition was manageable.

LOSING CONTROL

In 1993, Carla and her husband, Scott, celebrated the birth of their first child, a healthy baby girl. But pregnancy brought with it unforeseen problems. After her daughter, Kelsey, was born, the hormone levels in Carla's body changed. These changes made controlling her seizures more difficult.

For six years Carla's doctors worked to find the right medications and dosages that her body needed to control her epilepsy. Despite their efforts her seizures became more frequent and more intense.

"By the year 2000, my body was out of control. I was having seizures on a daily basis," says Carla. "I truly felt that my life was coming to a halt and the seizures were taking over. Desperate for answers to help my seizure problem, my daughter Kelsey and I prayed to God for help in dealing with seizures. In July 2000, Jesus answered my prayers when my sister-in-law and I were searching the Internet.

DISCOVERING A NEW OPTION

Searching for information about epilepsy treatment on the Internet, Carla found details about epilepsy surgery being done at Mayo clinic for people whose seizures couldn't be controlled with medications or other techniques. She and Scott decided to travel to Rochester, MN to find out more.

After several appointments and a thorough evaluation of her condition, neurologists at Mayo clinic determined that Carl's seizures could be pinpointed to one area of her brain, the left temporal lobe, and it was very likely that surgery could correct the problem.

"During my initial consultations, Scott and I felt comfortable and confident that we made the right choice to come to Mayo clinic," says Carla. "My first impression was that the patient's interests and medical needs were the doctors' first priority."

LIVING A FULL LIFE

On November 7, 2000, Carla underwent surgery to remove scar tissue from the left temporal lobe of her brain that her physicians at Mayo believed was causing the seizures.

"That was a day to cherish for me and my family because it was an opportunity to have my life back," says Carla.

Since that day, Carla has been seizure free. In November 2002, she not only passed the two-year anniversary of her successful surgery, she also took her last dose of one of her anti-seizure medications.

"The past three years since having epilepsy surgery have been the best for me. I feel like a new person," says Carla. "The freedom from having seizures has allowed me to live my life to the fullest."

Let's Begin The Journey Together

1 My First Six Months

Surprise, surprise!

I was a happy and healthy baby girl.

My mom went to her doctor because she thought she had the flu. Doc chuckled with delight and said he was going to bring her a baby girl.

"I'm what?" she exclaimed. "You're pulling my leg!"

Months later, my mom and dad welcomed their third child, a healthy baby girl.

Mom told me that she always wanted two boys and two girls. They already had two boys, and now their first girl. Two years later, another boy was born. Mom had her four children, but one girl instead of two.

My older brothers polled their grade school classmates for girl names. Carla was the name they chose, and Carla is what my parents named me.

"For You formed my inward parts; You wove me in my mother's womb"

Psalm 139:13

Your Turn

What is your story? What circumstances led to your diagnosis?

2 First Response

How does a parent respond when a child has a seizure? I was six months old when a high fever triggered a seizure. Helpless and terrified, my parents rushed their lethargic and nearly unconscious baby the few blocks to the doctor.

In our small hometown of about 1,000 people, we were blessed to have a compassionate physician who knew what to do. Our family doctor telephoned the local Chevy dealer and asked for a fast vehicle to rush me, my mom, and my dad to St. Mary's Hospital in Centralia, Illinois.

Awaiting our arrival at the hospital was the specialist that my doctor called to help me. Testing was done. Mom and Dad were advised to watch my behavior for any differences.

I was too young to know what had happened to me and too little to express my feelings. After a few days in the hospital, I was diagnosed with febrile seizures and released to go home.

Doubt, fear, and worry plagued my parents. Mom and Dad prayed that God would help them through these uncertain times. And for the next year and a half, I was just fine. I was a happy and healthy toddler.

God grant me the Serenity to accept the things I cannot change ... the courage to change the things I can and the Wisdom to know the difference (Prayer of Serenity).

"Casting all your anxiety on Him, because He cares for you."

1 Peter 5:7

Your Turn

How has this situation affected your relationship with your family?

Keeping the Faith

3

Then my life changed.

When I was two years old, I developed meningitis. The accompanying high fever resulted in convulsions that sent me into a coma. The first coma lasted 18 hours. The second lasted 24.

When I woke from the coma, the doctors at St. John's Mercy Medical Center diagnosed seizures and epilepsy resulting from the meningitis. They also found scar damage to the brain's left temporal lobe.

God, give us parents the strength and wisdom to get through these uncertain times (James 1:6).

Help us to train up our children in the way they should go (Proverbs 22:6).

Your Turn

When did life change for you?

4 — Grade School Years

From the first day of kindergarten, school was fun. I enjoyed my school experience. The first four years were easy transitions for me.

But in fifth grade, all that changed.

I remember it like a sad dream. I lost my place in the class as my teacher helped me pack my books. While the classmates I'd shared my days with remained together, my desk was moved to a corner room on the other side of school.

Why me? What is wrong with me? I was confused as these questions raced through my mind.

My new classroom was the resource room for assisted learning and special education. I was one of ten students in this class. After some time, I adjusted to the change. I felt more at ease and less overwhelmed in the smaller setting than I had in the larger regular class.

Learning became more difficult as I entered the higher grades. The hardest part was adjusting to change. During this time, my medicines for seizures were adjusted and another pill was added at lunch time.

Looking back thirty years at grade school, those moments of change were huge, but now I am encouraged by the results. Grade school years were great. However, the scars remain from watching other children mock students with a disability. Or poke fun at students who were not as quick to respond to the words of other kids.

My biggest challenge in school was to be like the other children. To be accepted by my peer group. To be seen as a person and friend. I longed for classmates to overlook what made me different. All I wanted was to run and play and have fun like the others.

"The words of a whisperer are like dainty morsels, And they go down into the innermost parts of the body.

Proverbs 18:8

Your Turn

What was your grade school experience? How did your condition affect your early school years?

5 Pressure Cooker

Graduation from grade school was a big moment in time. All 40 eighth graders were together as classmates for the last time. The big decision was where did I want to go to high school?

We had two great high schools in the nearby town, one private and one public. Some of my friends were going to the private school. Others chose the public campus. The public school offered a certified nurse's aide certificate if I completed all the nursing and medical classes. Because I planned to get my training in nursing, I attended the public school.

My cousin, who was more like a sister, helped me break out of my cocoon. "Smile," she coached. "Say hi to everybody. Be nice, and then you won't get tossed in the trash can." She was a senior when I was freshman. Her words of advice helped me talk to others and meet new people. Starting over in a new school, beginning a new adventure was exciting. My freshman year was the best.

In my sophomore year, I entered the driver education classroom and found a seat. I was just sitting down when the student next to me announced, "I am not sitting by you. You have seizures and I don't want to get them." Shocked, speechless, and embarrassed, I wanted to crawl under the desk and hide. I had to think fast – never my strong suit. "Seizures are not contagious," I said. "You can't get them from sitting next to me or sharing my drink. I take medicines for seizures and I can do the same things you do, including driving."

Saying those words restored my shaken confidence. The entire class had listened to our exchange. Apparently the student next to me had spoken for many of them. They appeared more at ease after my explanation.

"A man has joy in an apt answer, And how delightful is a timely word!"

Proverbs 15:23

Your Turn

The insensitive comments of those who don't understand can be embarrassing. When did you have to explain your condition to others?

6 What Others Think

Then came my hardest challenge. As a high school junior, my nursing training required going to the hospital to learn medical techniques and observations.

My instructor questioned my ability to do these clinicals. How could I convince my instructor that I was okay to do the medical requirements? Overhearing the comments and speculations of others was painful. It hurt deeply when they voiced their doubts about my capabilities and offered an abundance of 'what if' scenarios that always left me in a bad light.

How should I respond? I made the choice not to let their misgivings hold me back. I determined to move forward. I had to press past the areas that were hard to change.

I hope I never hold anyone back from achieving their dreams. I will do my best to turn negative moments into positive memories. I will strive to build others up, not tear them down — (Carla).

"God is our refuge and strength a very present help in trouble"

Psalm 46:1.

Your Turn

How do the negative assumptions of others regarding your abilities affect you? How would you like to respond to these situations in the future?

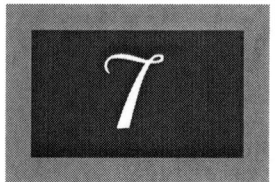

Why Me?

Why do I have to have this problem? Why do I have to deal with the social dilemmas when I have a seizure in public? Why can't I be like everyone else?

"Why me" was really a concern during my school years when I was searching for my niche and social peers. I was already out of sync in the class from the social stigma I felt. Twenty years later I discovered that some people never thought I was different after all. It is hard to be different. Having big brothers helped with much of the social and school issues.

Why do I have an awkward limp with my hip sticking out? Why do they call me names when my real name is Carla? Why do they call me 'spell' and mock my seizures?

I just wanted to be like the others. One day at school I remember having a turn around in my thinking when I realized that there were others who are worse off than me. I made my mind up to not let others hold me back.

Don't belittle to be little (Psalm 19:14).

"The steps of a good man are established by the Lord: and He delights in his way"

Psalm 37:23.

Your Turn

When do you ask the, "Why me?"

Cutting The Caffeine

During my teen and adult years, giving up my favorite soda was tough. My daily intake of three to six was not good for me. I had to make the choice to listen to my neurologists both at Barnes Hospital in St. Louis and again at the Mayo Clinic. I needed to limit caffeine due to the numerous seizures I was having.

Had it not been out of balance in my life, I wouldn't have been told twice by two different specialists. It helped keep the seizures under control when I limited caffeine and stress. It was within my power to limit items that stimulated the brain to cause seizure activity.

It took me seven months to eliminate the caffeine soda from my diet. It wasn't easy, but I did it. The headaches, jittering, and dizziness

disappeared when I stopped drinking caffeine sodas.

Have fun in life and enjoy all life's moments that you have been given.

"I can do all things through Him who strengthens me."
Philippians 4:13.

Your Turn

What habits are you continuing that are harmful to you? Do you think the rewards are worth the hard work of eliminating them from your life?

Alcohol And Drugs Don't Mix

Taking seizure medicines since age two, I learned the importance of taking care of myself as I grew older. The effects of taking medicines were discussed many times with my doctor who wanted me to understand that alcohol could weaken the effectiveness of the seizure medications.

During my teen years and early twenties, drinking was the social activity at clubhouses, picnics, and road parties. I tried social drinking but never liked the taste of beer. Drinking and late night hours led to a relapse in my body. Occasionally, I experienced major setbacks that involved seizures of maximum intensity, leaving me tired and worn out.

I decided to do the right thing for myself. I became the designated driver. I had fun without drinking, and felt much better.

I deserve to take care of myself, to take the right steps to getting myself better than ever before. I will do this for me rather than do what others want me to do.

"The Lord will guard your going out and your coming in from this time forth and forever.

Psalm 121:8.

Your Turn

How can you creatively stay included in your social settings with peers without compromising your own health?

Insecurities

Some days, I felt strong and able to accomplish anything. Other days, the seizures left me feeling tense, weak, and insecure. Why would I feel this way one day and another day feel just the opposite? Not having control over my body caused me to question my ability to hold a full time job. I cringed at the thought of making a scene in public.

My doctor assured, "Carla, your chances of having a seizure while on the seizure medicines is as likely as someone having a heart attack." His words helped me put my insecurity into a positive focus and perspective.

"Now may the God of hope fill you with all joy and peace in believing, so that you will abound in hope by the power of the Holy Spirit."

Romans 15:3

Your Turn

What insecurities have you had to overcome? What repeating tape of uneasy questions plays over and over in your mind?

Medications - The Good, The Bad

Seizure medications may affect bone calcium. Seizure medications affect the vitamin D, an essential needed to build bones. Though I'd taken these medications since I was an infant, some 40 years, I was never aware that this could cause bone density loss. I was beginning to find joy in learning how to take care of my new healthy body.

My doctors and specialists advised me to make a few changes to build bone mass:

- Eliminate refined sugars like junk food
- Regularly do weight bearing exercise such as walking
- Get three serving of calcium daily
- Limit soda intake due the effect phosphoric acid has on the bones

Based on doctor recommendations, I also added a supplement to my diet called Metagenics.

"Be gracious to me, O Lord, for I am pining away; Heal me, O Lord, for my bones are dismayed."

Psalm 6:2

Your Turn

Which of these recommendations will you incorporate today? Which will you incorporate next?

12

Searching For A Miracle

On the eve of a new millennium, I needed a miracle. The year 2000 had just begun and I prayed I would make it through New Year's Eve.

I was rapidly growing weaker. I was helpless to even drive myself home from the local pharmacist three blocks away where I went to get seizure medicines refilled before the holiday began. I was tired and nauseous. My arms and legs felt jittery and mushy like Santa's poetic bowl full of jelly. My whole body was shutting down and I needed help to get home.

Brenda and Carol at the pharmacy drove me home. My sister-in-law, a nurse, helped me contact my specialist. Offices were closed for the holiday but I needed to know what to do with my next dose of medicine. When the doctor called back, we decreased both seizure medicines, one I'd been on for twenty years.

There were blizzard conditions as I spoke to my neurologist on the phone. He said I could come to the hospital an hour away, but my husband told me to hang tough. I went to sleep feeling scared and uneasy. What I was going through felt like the hardest battle. Weak and nauseous, I had to trust God to get me through the night. My husband was my angel from God to get me through the storm.

"Be still and know that I am God;"

Psalm 46:10 (NKJV)

Your Turn

When was your toughest battle? Who did God send to help you through?

13 One Day At A Time

A new year and a new hope. January 1, 2000. I made through the darkest hours of my life. It had been a difficult night but a new day arrived. As the New Year unfolded around the world, I woke feeling excitement and relief that the night had come and gone. The new day was without any problems from the medicines or seizures.

The road to adjusting medications was bumpy. Finding the right levels of medicines and keeping the seizures at bay was the main concern on my mind. The limb numbness, tingly, jelly feeling felt better overnight. Scared and unsure about changing medicines, I was emotionally weak. I needed answers medically, mentally, and emotionally.

I can truly say that only by a higher source of power did I get through. I walk by faith and not by sight.

"I have fought the good fight, I have finished the course, I have kept the faith;"

2 Timothy 4:7.

Your Turn

Who is your strength in times of trouble?

14   Major Medical Setbacks

The first three months of 2000 were the hardest times of my life besides the misdiagnosis I endured in 1994 after the birth of our daughter. I was completely worn out mentally, physically, emotionally, and psychologically.

My medical options looked grim. I truly felt overwhelmed, and overexerted as I tried to keep going. The toll my condition took on my husband, daughter, and my family grieved my heart.

My sister-in-law told me of a neurologist who came to our local hospital. My brother drove me to the neurologist to seek a second opinion on my medicines. She helped me reduce the medicines that caused the reaction on New Years Eve. She began a new medicine to replace the other, and added a second medicine to help stop the seizure when it occurred.

"What are my options, Doc?"

She gave me information and contact numbers. She described a surgery to install a magnet into the neck that stopped seizures from occurring when the patient pressed the defibrillator. It blocked the misfire from occurring. It was an option but I decided that was not my choice.

I found strength through prayer. I asked God for direction. Doors opened and opportunities of hope began to flood in.

"Ask and it will be given to you; seek, and you will find; knock, and it will be opened to you"

Matthew 7:7

Your Turn

What options have you found?

Emotionally And Mentally Unfit

During the bleak year of 2000, my family members and my doctor advised me to seek counseling. I was obsessed over my feelings and emotions. I overstressed even little things that were happening to my body. I felt completely helpless, hopeless, and distraught.

The neurologist gave me the name of the clinical psychologist. I was a basket case to say the least. Having a full blown panic attack, numb from head to toe, short of breath, intensely fearful, and scared to be home alone, I sought professional help. At the weakest point in my life, I sought wise counsel.

"Seek the Lord and His Strength; Seek His face continually."

Psalm 105:4

Your Turn

Have you sought wise counsel through a professional?

16 Another Seizure

The day began great. It was a day to look forward to, and I was excited to see what would unfold. I was grateful to be alive.

I learned to hold onto those thoughts during the tough times that blew me off course. When hard times hit out of the blue for no reason known to me, those uneasy urges in my body began to fester. The bad odors and tastes reminded me I did not have control over my body's reaction to these seizures. I felt helpless, uneasy, afraid of the unknown, and at the mercy of others.

After my daughter was born, I was one of the 20 percent of people diagnosed with epilepsy that was hard to control following pregnancy. After giving birth, medicines proved less effective to control the seizures due to hormonal imbalances.

During the first six years after Kelsey was born, I dealt with medicines, seizures, loss of driving privileges, and having six to twelve seizures a day. I cried out to God for answers to my overwhelming health needs.

Healing came when I followed where God led.

"And my soul is greatly dismayed; But you, O Lord how long? Return, O Lord, rescue my soul; Save me because of Your loving kindness."

Psalm 6:3-4.

Your Turn

It can be tempting to give up when we feel tired and overwhelmed. Where is God urging you to go next?

What If I Have A Seizure?

For ten terrible years, my thoughts replayed the same question. What if I have a seizure today? Though the surgery had eliminated the seizures, my mind still continually asked the question quietly and countless times a day.

What if the past comes back to haunt me? What could I do to change this panic inducing thought pattern?

"Ninety percent worry and only ten percent problem," my friend said. "Focus on the promises."

I discussed this issue with my counselor during my recovery after brain surgery. He advised me to act like a lawyer arguing a defense case in court.

In my journal, I recorded the pros and cons, focused on the positives and weighed the truth and facts. I began to speak healing words of encouragement, affirmation, faith and scripture over my situation.

God, help me to focus on you and not the battles of my mind that try to keep me from receiving your promises (Carla).

Your Turn

What negative words do you rehearse in your mind? Make a list of positive truths you will tell yourself instead, beginning today.

18 My Pain Is Their Pain

During the intense battles with seizures, those normal daily tasks of driving, chores, errands, holding down a job, taking care of my family, and taking care of myself were complicated with adjusting to the changes in lifestyle and medicines. With the additional medical bills mounting, as a wife and mother, I could see the hurt and feel the pain my husband and daughter were enduring.

My husband and my daughter were unsure of what to do. How would we deal with mom unable to drive? Trying to remain strong for my family was an additional responsibility. How could I keep my faith and inner spirit positive when my heart was heavy and burdened?

Friends offered to take my daughter to gymnastics. While my own confidence plummeted and I doubted myself, the fact was that I needed to rely on friends and family to help me do what I couldn't do for myself.

Recalling those challenging times, I am more appreciative of the gifts God has given to me. I want to keep my heart open to others who are struggling as I once did.

"But to each one is given the manifestation of the Spirit for the common good."

1 Corinthians 12:7.

Your Turn

What gifts has God given to you? How can you help another who is struggling?

19 Danger On The Road

Driving that once had seemed safe and fun, now appeared to be a danger. The threat of seizures meant I was a threat on the road. Losing driving privileges was a matter of safety for me, my family, and for other innocent drivers on and off the road.

Still, losing driving privileges was emotionally and mentally anguishing. Additionally, those three years without a driver's license made it hard to maintain a job, raise a family, and keep socially connected with the outside world. I valued my family, friends, and neighbors more than ever before.

This situation forced me to rethink a lot of things I took for granted. I fought the urge to blame myself for the situation. I had to find creative ways to make a living from my home.

Previously I hadn't considered how this stigma affected people until I experienced it myself. Though it was heart wrenching, I knew giving up the ability to drive was the right thing to do for all of us. I gave up a dear freedom. Walking, ride sharing, and doing work from home was necessary for me.

Better to be safe than sorry.

"How blessed is the man who finds wisdom And the man who gains understanding."

Provers 3:12

Your Turn

What freedoms or common privileges have you had to give up? What creative ways have you developed to compensate?

20 Life Disrupted

Heavily distracted in my thinking, wildly racing thoughts pierced my emotions. Feeling out of control, and anxious, the overwhelming burdens were heavy in my heart. My medical issues reduced my life to a half. My license was suspended due to the seizures. I had to tell our five year old daughter that she could no longer take gymnastics because her mommy no longer has the common privilege of driving. It was heartbreaking to me and crushing to her at such a young age. I needed to seek help and counseling. Would I hire a driver to take me places? Could I afford counseling? Would it work?

How was I going to raise my family? I noticed my husband and child sensed that I was not feeling well and they tried to remain strong for me.

How was I going to make these decisions? What should I do? How could I cope? How would I keep Kelsey in the social settings she needed, like preschool? How could I not burden my family?

I discussed these topics with my counselor, and began to see God's hand at work in my life. People came and helped me through my battles during these hardest of times.

"Trust in the Lord with all your heart And do not lean on your own understanding. In all your ways acknowledge Him and He will make your paths straight."

1 Peter 5:7.

Your Turn

What are your biggest concerns?

21 — My Four-Legged Friend

Dogs that are trained to assist people with seizures can predict and alert their owners nearly twenty minutes before a seizure occurs. These four legged companions can be a lifesaver for people with seizures. During those long, confusing days when I was unable to drive or work due to my condition, my golden retriever, Bucky was my security on the days that I was home alone and driving privileges suspended and seizures medications being adjusted.

What a comfort to reach out and place my hand on his warm and furry head. He was always eager to receive my affection and his presence had a calming affect on my worried mind. Bucky's bright eyes spoke confidence. Knowing he could sense a brewing occurrence was a reflection of the Lord's presence. My God, who knit me together, also knew my future. Nothing was a surprise to Him.

Bucky knew his purpose. He was there for me. Fully there, cheerfully there. He lived in the moment and gave one hundred percent of himself to his calling. A dog is man's (or woman's) best friend. In my case, my dog was also a lifeline, companion, and lifesaver.

Would a dog be a comforting companion for you? Here are resources to help you explore this option.

1. Canine Assistants: (1- 800-771-7221), www.canineassistants.org
2. Delta Society: www.deltalsociety.org
3. Assistance Dogs International Inc.: www.adionline.org
4. American Dog Trainers Network: inch.com/dog/training.html
5. International Association of Assistance Dog Partners: www.iaddp.org

Neurology Now Magazine, page 46, July/August 2006

"But the Lord is faithful, and He will strengthen and protect you from the evil one."

II Thessalonians 3:3.

Your Turn

How has your dog or other pet proven to be a help in time of need for you?

22   There Is Hope!

Hope is the source that brings happiness, a peace to my inner self. What I dream about and focus my attention on is what I desire to do in my heart. I can use my talents and abilities to help others.

I searched the Internet for answers concerning my unbearable and debilitating ups and downs with medicines in hopes of keeping seizures at bay. I needed to function and carry out my daily tasks of raising a family, having a career, and hopefully being able to drive again.

In my 35 years of seizures, I never thought I would be as desperate for help as I was in 2000. My hopelessness began as my body shut down from the side effects of the various medicines, anxiety, and stress.

My hope came alive when I had the opportunity to have the seizures eliminated. By living those hard, uncertain years, I have a taste of the pain others experience in their lives. Helping others have hope and comfort brings me joy.

"Who comforts us in all our affliction so that we will be able to comfort those who are in any affliction with the comfort with which we ourselves are comforted by God."

2 Corinthians 1:4

Your Turn

What is your source of hope? How can you be a source of hope for another?

23 Miracles Happen

My miracle story is having my prayers answered. To find the medical help that gave me an opportunity to have my life back without the struggles and difficulties that were affecting me and my family. I wanted to be more independent so I could give my child opportunities to do things a kid should do.

God answered my prayers the day I called the Mayo Clinic, and again six months later when I visited Rochester, Minnesota in October of 2000. It was the best day of my life when Dr. Gregory Cascino told me he could help. I was thrilled when he began the evaluation tests, confirmed a diagnosis, and I met the team of specialists who were pivotal in my journey. These were all parts of a miracle in the making.

Having another chance at life is a miracle itself.

"A cheerful heart is good medicine, but a crushed spirit dries up the bones."

Proverbs 17:22.

Your Turn

Is there a miracle in the making on your horizon? Who are the people who are part of your miracle?

24 Epilepsy Evaluation Center

At my first visit with the neurologist, they evaluated the MRI results of my brain. The nurse advised me on the upcoming stay at the Epilepsy Evaluation Center. She explained that during the stay in the Center, I would be monitored by 24 hour video, reduced and eliminated off my seizure medication, deprived of sleep, and have seizures induced. This would allow the staff to pinpoint the intensity and location of the seizures.

During the admission into the Evaluation Center at the Rochester Methodist Hospital at the Mayo Clinic, the first appointment was for an EEG (Electroencephalogram). Small electrode wires glued to my scalp recorded where in the brain the seizures began.

My first day in the evaluation center, I was advised not to get out of bed by myself. A nurse and physician were nearby at all times. I was deprived of sleep, and given exercises to induce the seizures to occur. Tuesday, Wednesday, and Thursday, I was in the Epilepsy Evaluation Center.

On the third day, Dr. So told me that they had pinpointed the seizure area of the brain. The seizures I was experiencing could cause my heart to skip a beat and lead to cardiac arrest. The situation was operable.

I was excited and relieved to hear that good news. I consulted with Dr. Cascino after being discharged from the Center. Prior to surgery, there would be a consultation with the Neuropsychologist, psychological and memory and peripheral vision testing, as well as a pre-surgery consultation with the surgeon.

"I wish I could talk to someone who had the surgery and could answer my questions about the surgery," I told the doctor. He immediately opened his desk drawer and phoned a lady from Indiana. A music instructor, she'd had the surgery nine years ago. It was like I'd known her all my life. She was a teacher, I was a teacher. She answered my questions, gave pointers, and assured me I was not alone. At that point, I felt the peace and comfort to pursue the surgery.

Dr. Cascino had some questions of his own. "Do you feel your life is coming to a halt?"

Epilepsy Evaluation Center continued

"Yes," I answered.

"Do you feel that seizures are keeping you from living life?"

"Yes."

"Is your family affected by the ongoing seizures?"

"Yes."

He reiterated that he was not making my decisions for me, but merely presenting the best options available for my medical concerns and possible care. He had done that ten times over. In that desperate moment in my life, he supplied the best hope for me yet.

As we went home for a week before returning to the Mayo Clinic for more pre-surgery tests and evaluation, I held onto hope. Back in Illinois, I watched my favorite TV series, ER. It was like seeing my life played out on the program as the television character, Mark, was also being tested for seizure surgery in the hospital. It helped me to know I was not alone. I am forever grateful for all the help and hope that these people have given me.

"I would have despaired unless I had believed that I would see the goodness of the Lord in the land of the living."

Psalm 27:13

Turn the page for Your Turn

Your Turn

Have you seen your situation mirrored in someone else's life? When have you been assured that you are not alone?

Your Turn

25 Medical History Journal

Keeping a journal helped my doctor and specialists know pertinent information about my medical condition. The journal recorded both current and past seizure patterns and how the seizures were treated medically.

I wrote details that others had observed regarding my seizures as well as notes about how I felt before and after events. It was too much to remember, but easy enough to jot several lines periodically. That information proved helpful to the doctors as we progressed through the evaluations. *Every little bit helps and you are worth every little bit. Life is too precious to miss out on the opportunity.*

"Then the Lord answered me and said, Record the vision And inscribe it on tablets, That the one who reads it may run."

Habakkuk 2:2

Your Turn

Do you keep a journal? It doesn't have to be daily or extensive or time consuming. A few lines about your physical symptoms will help your doctor. A line or two about your emotional and spiritual condition will allow you to track your own progress.

26   Tests, Tests, Tests

Neurological examinations included testing my reflexes, muscle tone and strength, the function of my senses, and my gait, posture, coordination, and balance. My doctor asked questions to test my thinking, judgment, and memory.

Blood was drawn to test for chemical imbalances that may cause seizures. A simple needle stick in the right or left arm drew blood into the tube for these tests.

An EEG recorded the electrical activity of my brain. An EEG helped determine what type of seizures or epilepsy I had and from which part of the brain seizures may start. Lying down during the half hour procedure, between 16 and 30 small electrodes were attached to my scalp.

Remaining still, I was asked to breathe deeply and steadily for several minutes. Sometimes, I stared at a patterned board. At other times, a light was flashed in my eyes. These actions were intended to stimulate my brain in ways that could be seen on the EEG. The electrodes picked up the brain's electrical impulses and sent them to the EEG machine, which recorded the brain waves.

A computerized tomography, or CT test, produced detailed cross-sectional images of my brain. These images may reveal abnormalities in brain structure, including tumors, cysts, strokes, or tangled blood vessels.

A magnetic resonance imaging or MRI produced images of my brain through a powerful magnetic field and radio waves. Like CT scans, MRI images may reveal abnormalities in brain structure. Lying on my back for about 45 minutes, the MRI filmed my brain. The time it takes for the tests are minimal for the results of what is needed to help them help you.

"The steadfast of mind You will keep in perfect peace, because he trusts in You."

Isaiah 26:3

Your Turn

What tests have you undergone to find answers to your condition?

Auras

An aura is "an odd smell, taste, sound, feeling, or having a feeling of having already experienced what is happening" (page. 526, American College of Physicians Complete Home Medical Guide).

Many auras I had were warning signals my body sent as the warning sign of a seizure about to begin. They began with the smell of bacon or a bad breath odor that lingered in the roof of my mouth and in my nose. Sometimes, I had just the aura without a seizure. I'd wait to see what would happen and how hard it would be. When the moments of just an aura occurred I felt a huge relief, grateful that it all ended quickly and quietly.

After surgery for seizures, I never experienced another foul odor or smell again.

"I press on towards the goal for the prize of the upward call of God in Christ Jesus."

Philippians 3:14.

Your Turn

What symptoms, such as auras, alert you to a potential episode?

The Big Day

There was hope for me on Tuesday morning, November 7, 2000. History was made on this day as the presidential election unfolded. However, another major event happened to me. I elected to pursue a chance to have my life back. I had brain surgery.

I hoped this drastic procedure would completely eliminate the epilepsy and seizures. At the least, it would reduce and control the seizures that held me back from living my life to the fullest.

I awoke with great expectations at 5:00 a.m. in our hotel room in Rochester, Minnesota. There was some preparation to do before the surgery. A distinguished looking gentleman chauffeured me and my husband in a green shuttle bus across town from the Holiday Inn South to the Mayo clinic surgical center.

I was excited and hopeful for a new beginning.

"Don't be afraid; just believe,"

Mark 5:36

Your Turn

What, if any, medications, surgeries, techniques, etc. have you tried and how have the results affected your life?

Brain Surgery

The nurse called my name. I kissed and hugged my husband tightly; tears of joy and love filled both our eyes. I felt God's hand in this. I had peace, joy, and a sense that everything would be okay.

Dressing in surgical clothes, I was excited to have an opportunity to be better. The seizures were strong enough to potentially cause a sudden cardiac arrest.

I saw a man coming down the hallway with a cup of coffee in his hand. "There's the neurosurgeon that will do your surgery," the nurse said.

In the surgery room, the medical staff made me comfortable and the anesthesiologist told me to count backwards from 99. I remember getting to 90.

The neurosurgeon removed a half dollar size of scar tissue from the left temporal lobe of my brain. That small area of my body had caused multiple seizures nearly every day of my life since I was two.

"Let all who seek You rejoice and be glad in You; Let those who love Your salvation say continually, 'The Lord be magnified!'"

Psalm 40:16

Your Turn

Have you experienced a turning point in your health, what was it?

30 — Intensive Care Unit
Recovery

Six hours later, I woke up from the surgery. Through the fog, I was blurrily aware as the nurses wheeled me from recovery to the Intensive Care Unit.

At dinner time, I opened my eyes to see my husband next to my bed. He looked tired. I was happy and pleased to see him. The nurses assured him I was fine and told him to go back to the hotel and rest.

Wires, drainage tubes, and gauze were wrapped around my head. Hoses for circulation were attached to my legs and feet. Every hour, the nurse monitored my heart and brain function. Swelling and fluid on the brain were concerns. With all the fine nurses and doctors, everything went well.

Before the evening was over, my nurse came in to turn off the TV and tell me I hadn't missed a thing. There was no winner yet in the presidential election. We had a great chuckle and even though I couldn't laugh out loud, it was a great moment.

"He makes me lie down in green pastures."

Psalm 23:2.

Your Turn

What moments for you have been great?

First Morning After Surgery

31

The new day of my new life began at 6:00 a.m. The neurologist came to see me in the Intensive Care Unit. This doctor had seen me through my three days in the epilepsy evaluation center where they pinpointed the area of the brain where the numerous seizures occurred.

The neurologist checked my vital signs and monitored how I did when I got out of bed. If I could sit in a chair, and hold down food without dizziness or nausea, I could graduate from ICU to the recovery floor.

We discussed my options, the possibility of eliminating one of my medications. I was cautious. He was empathetic and respectful. That morning I was moved to the surgery recovery floor.

My head was wrapped in a cloth tunic, monitors and hoses were attached to the left side of my head. The skinny hoses drained fluids from my brain, alleviating swelling and pressure from the surgical area.

"You don't want to know how bad you looked," my husband told me later. "I've never seen anything like it."

"Just a bad hair day," was my response. "It will be okay."

Laughter was the best medicine. It lightened the load for my body and soul. All was going well. I had made it 24 hours without any seizures.

"Our mouths were filled with laughter; our tongues were filled with songs of joy"

Psalm 126:2

Your Turn

Share some moments when laughter was good medicine for you.

32 — 48 Hours After Surgery

The success of the surgery was measured by the amount of time I went without seizures. My mind was clear as I talked with my sister-in-law Kathy on the phone. Kathy said she couldn't believe how healthy I sounded.

My cousin, Cindy called from back home in Illinois. She had a wig business and wanted to know if she needed to make a wig for my head after surgery. Amazingly, only an unnoticeable strip of hair had been removed beneath the rest of my hair.

My vision was my biggest concern. The picture on the wall of my room appeared to be outlines of a cow. It scared me. The doctor assured me this would improve in time. My one eye was swollen. I was given a medicine called Heparin to reduce the swelling in my brain and my eye. Applying ice packs to my eye, and the headaches on the left side of my temporal lobe, was helpful.

My room was on the eighth floor, directly across from the nurses' station. With the nurse's help, I got up for a walk. I walked slowly with the help of my husband, or a walker, or a nurse until I felt secure to do it alone. Starting out, I was dizzy, woozy, uneasy, and worn out. My first walk was slow and short. Each day was better than the day before.

"For who has despised the day of small things..."

Zechariah 4:10

Your Turn

Where has progress seemed slow, but steady in your life?

33   Will I Stay Or Will I Go?

Three days after surgery, I was scheduled to be discharged from the hospital to begin our journey back home from Minnesota to Trenton, Illinois. I was feeling somewhat better. The swelling in my eye was going down. And the best part – still no seizures! Yeah!

The doctor had written my discharge papers and prepared instructions for my three month recovery at home. I was told to rest. I was not to drive, not to lift anything over ten pounds, not to bend and pick up objects causing any strain on my body, or to exert myself. All of these would adversely affect my recovery.

Within hours of being told I could go home, the neurosurgeon came to my room to see how I was doing. Thank God he came when he did. In those few hours, I began to feel ill, nauseous, and weak. I was in no shape to travel eight hours.

My body was reacting to the medicine prescribed to reduce swelling. The doctor told me not to worry.

"Just rest," he said. "We'll try again tomorrow. After we see how you feel, we will decide when you can go home."

"So do not worry about tomorrow, for tomorrow will care for itself. Each day has enough trouble of its own."

Matthew 6:34

Your Turn

Can you rest and leave tomorrow's worries to tomorrow?

34 Going Home

Four days after brain surgery, the eye swelling had gone down tremendously. I was able to shower, and have clean hair before I left. To keep my head warm and cover the eight staples in my scalp, and I wore a soft green cap.

Feeling and looking much better than the day before, I was taken by wheelchair from the room. I said goodbye to the nurses, thanking them for their excellent help and support. The staff had been great to me from that first day in October when I walked into the Mayo Clinic until the day I left a month later.

Armed with a pain prescription for the headaches that could possibly feel sharp and piercing, my husband and I left the hospital and headed home.

In the back of our burgundy suburban were blankets, and pillows for a makeshift bed. I rested and slept while Scott drove us back to Illinois. A few hours later we stopped to stretch and treat ourselves to a root beer float and chicken nuggets at the A&W restaurant.

Although we planned to drive four hours, we drove two more and stayed at a hotel in Mt. Pleasant, Iowa. We were halfway home.

"Come to me, all who are weary and heavy-laden, and I will give you rest."

Matthew 11:28

Your Turn

What does rest look like for you?

35 Home Sweet Home

Seven days after surgery. To help me keep the staples in my head dry, Kathy came to wash and style my hair for Kelsey's seventh birthday party that night. I was excited to see my whole family together again for the first time since my surgery. I felt like a whole new person. I felt really good inside. No one could tell I had brain surgery just six days ago.

The little things others did to help were Godly blessings to me. God knew what I needed and how to bring those sincere gestures at the right moment. God gave me freedom. Every day without seizures is another victory.

"But thanks be to God, who gives us the victory through our Lord Jesus Christ."

1 Corinthians 15:57

Your Turn

What gestures, small and large, have others done that remind you that God remembers you and loves you?

Psychogenic Seizures

After having brain surgery, I began my three month recovery back home which is eight hours away from the Mayo Clinic. All went well until I began to have feelings in the left temporal lobe of my brain. It was an oozing sensation, like a warm liquid was slowly moving down in my skull and out my ear.

By phone, I consulted with the surgeon's nurse. My home physician checked my ears and nose for any oozing. Nothing was noticeable. I took their advice to rest, relax, and try not to worry. Tired and drained, I had a hard time discerning what was important and what was not.

During the first twelve weeks after surgery, I wrote my thoughts and prayed for answers. At the advice of my doctor, I went for counseling.

The clinical psychologist at our local hospital helped me. The doctor and my neurologist diagnosed psychogenic seizures. Psychogenic or fake seizures seem to be caused by stressful psychological experiences or emotional trauma. Psychogenic non epileptic seizures are one way that the body indicates excessive stress. Known as pseudo seizures or hysterical seizures, these were a problem of my mind.

Journaling, counseling, social support, and prayer were key to healing. A friend shared a book by Charles Capps titled, *God's Creative Power of Healing*. Quoting scriptures aloud, my faith grew and the situation began to turn around. God helped me have clear thoughts and a clear mind.

"For God has not given us a spirit of fear, but of power and of love and of a sound mind."

2 Timothy 1:7 (NKJ)

Your Turn

Which scriptures provide comfort and assurance for you? What new passage will you commit to memory this week?

37 — Three Month Check-Up

It was time for my three month check-up. The first thirty days after surgery were rough. The second thirty were better. The last thirty was the best of all. I was feeling better day by day. The rocky road was beginning to smooth out. Doctor's orders to me were no driving, no lifting anything over ten pounds, get plenty of rest, and take medicines for severe headaches if needed.

"You are a home run!" declared the neurosurgeon. During my check-up, the doctor who had done my surgery evaluated my notes. He told me that things had settled down from the possible seizures I had been experiencing.

"Throw away the old book and start a new one," the neurosurgeon stated. "Enjoy your new life. You are not sick anymore!" An astonishing, heartfelt, breathtaking joy washed over me. A sigh of relief, a leap of gladness, and a burst of faith rose within me. It was a day of hope. Priceless.

"I will be glad and rejoice in Your love, for You saw my affliction and knew the anguish of my soul."

Psalm 31:7 (NIV 2011)

Your Turn

Hope is a powerful emotion. What is the source of your hope?

38 Anxiety Attacks

Back home after surgery, I began to feel seizure-like sensations. There was a rush down my arms, body chills, numbness from head to toe, and feeling short of breath. Dr. Cascino explained that about ten percent of the people who have the surgery experience panic attacks.

I was overwhelmed by the sensations so similar to a seizure. Taking the advice of my doctors, I sought professional counseling. Three years of counseling with the clinical psychologist and support from my neurologist helped me progress past the fear, panic, and anxiety. I learned to retrain my thoughts away from being guarded and jumpy toward uncertain sensations.

After having seizures since preschool age, I thought it would be an easy thing to finally move beyond the past. As delighted as I was to have new life and new hope for the future, I had to learn how to refocus my mind away from constantly thinking "what if."

It was freeing to work past those areas anchored in the past. Anxiety felt like I was losing control. Journaling, relaxation tapes, doing things I enjoyed, helping others, prayer, and nurturing hope were tools that helped me.

> "And the peace of God, which surpasses all comprehension, will guard your hearts and your minds In Christ Jesus."
>
> Philippians 4:7

Your Turn

What tools have you developed to combat anxiety?

Living Life To The Fullest

Living life to the fullest was the farthest goal from my thoughts when my first priority was to get through one day without having seizures. Following the surgery, years of counseling and changing my thoughts were steps toward a bright future. It was time to embrace life.

Living with epilepsy, or any disability, doesn't mean we can't return to daily activities. God gave us the determination to fight the battles head on. Do not lie down and give up.

To start living, I had to step out of the small box that was my comfort zone. What would I like to accomplish in my life? What were my goals? What were my dreams and life passions? Now I could make a plan and work the plan.

Enjoy life to the fullest. You deserve the best.

"Commit your works to the Lord And your plans will be established."

Proverbs 16:3

Your Turn

What are your passions? What are your talents and gifts that you can share with others?

40 Is This Normal Jerking?

It was early morning. As I woke to a new day, a chill ran down my spine. I felt an occasional jerking in my leg, stomach, and back.

Are these seizures? Panic threatened to overwhelm me. My mind wanted to run with the thoughts that something was wrong. Was this just a nerve impulse reaction?

Being aware of my surroundings, of where I was and what I was doing reassured me that all was well. I was comforted by the fact that this twitching was in my lower leg and stomach. When it happened as I woke, it resembled the seizures before my surgery for epilepsy. When fear flooded my mind, I reined my thoughts in the way they should go. I countered with comforting words of scripture. The Word of God delivered relief and assurance to my body, soul, and spirit in any moment of my day.

Myoclonic Seizure – a sudden brief, massive muscle jerk that may involve the whole body or parts of the body. May cause a person to spill what they are holding or fall off the chair. No first aid is needed, but should be given medical evaluation, (Seizure Recognition and First Aid, 2003 Epilepsy Foundation of America).

Similarly, I experienced jerks and motions in my sleep, and awake, while lying down relaxing. I asked my doctor about these and I felt comforted to know that all was well, and normal.

To maintain a positive outlook, I put the past behind. Every day is a blessing. I decided to make the best of every moment of each new day, even the days that began with a tremor and fearful wondering.

"Finally, brethren, whatever is true, whatever is honorable, whatever is right, whatever is pure, whatever is lovely, whatever is of good repute, if there is any excellence and if anything worthy of praise, dwell on these things."

Philippians 4:8.

Your Turn

What are you afraid of? How do you counter your fear?

41 Six Months After Surgery

May 2, 2001

Dear Dr. Gregory Cascino,

February - May 2001. I have not had any seizures, nor rush feelings in my stomach, nauseousness, or other symptoms that feel like a seizure. No loss of consciousness. I have been doing really well with the anxiety. Those feelings of prickly stomach have dissipated. I am still seeing the clinical psychologist Dr. Abramson, and feel ready to move past the weekly visit.

I returned to substitute teaching, usually three days a week, sometimes four days. I have returned to normal daily activities and my energy level has increased as well. My confidence and abilities seem to be better. I don't feel mentally foggy, and I do not need the naps anymore.

Never before have I been so full of life and energy. Thank you and God bless,

Carla Huelsmann

"Being confident of this very thing, that He who has begun a good work in you will complete it until the day of Jesus Christ."

Philippians 1:6 (NKJV)

Your Turn

Looking back over the past six months, what improvements do you see?

One Year Check-Up

October 1, 2001

Dear Dr. Gregory Cascino,

This letter is to update you on my past five months of recovery.

I had a little scare this past summer when we were boating. I didn't have a seizure, but was in the wrong place at the wrong time when a full 12 ounce can that was tossed to someone hit me in the back of the head. I put up my hand to block it and moved to avoid the impact, but it still hit me. My hand did take the brunt of it. I went to the doctor that week for a check-up and he said all was fine.

To my knowledge, I have not had any seizures. I am still seeing Dr. Abramson, who has helped me to let go of the past thirty some years of anxiety and pseudo-auras. Thanks for working with him on my behalf.

My only complaint is headaches in that crease in my forehead or in the part of the temporal where it dents in from the surgery. They are not migraines. Though I do take naps, it is not a daily thing like it had been the first six months.

Carla Huelsmann

"The Lord will keep you from all harm- he will watch over your life".

Psalm 121:7 (NIV 2011)

Your Turn

Who would you like to thank for their help in your life?

Decreasing Medicines After Surgery

February 27, 2002

Dear Dr. Gregory Cascino,

It's been one year and three months since surgery. All is going well. To my knowledge, I have not had a single seizure. This is a milestone for me, the longest time without a seizure.

I believe that I am ready to decrease the Neurotin. I saw Dr. Abramson, Clinical Psychologist and he agrees I am ready to taper off the medicine.

I am currently taking Neurotin 300 mg. four times daily. I take one tablet at 9:00 a.m., 1:00 p.m., 5:00 p.m. and 9:00 p.m. This is so exciting to write this letter, and to look forward to no longer feeling drowsy.

Please call to tell me what you want me to do. I look forward to hearing from you. Thanks again for all you do.

God bless,
Carla Huelsmann

"My mouth will speak the praise of the Lord, And all flesh will bless His holy name forever and ever."

Psalm 145: 21

Your Turn

What is the next step you are ready to take?

44 Three Year Check-Up

December 1, 2003

Dr. Gregory Cascino,

This past year has been awesome! It was three years since surgery on November 7, 2000. I haven't had any seizures or pseudo auras during this year since my last check-up. You were right on during my last visit when you told me to throw away my seizure book. This has been my first full year off the second medicine, Neurontin, since November 17, 2003. Overall, I am less anxious and doing well. However, I do have some medical concerns:

Dr. Girgiss, Endocrinologist, told me that due to the low estrogen, and early menopause that I probably need estrogen. However, it may interfere with the Tegretal and the recovery of the surgery. Is this a concern given I have been seizure free since surgery? Dr. Girgiss said he would fax you a summary of this matter.

Dr. Garcia, MD, did blood work in August and September and found some levels out of range. I do recall I had the start of a sore throat at the time of the blood test. Could you please look at these results and tell me if there is anything we need to be concerned about?

Dr. Dermody tried to help before referring me to Dr. Girgiss. In February, 2002, I had a hot flash day. I had my last period that month. March, no period and first month reducing Neurontin. (Mar-Nov 02.) Summer 2002, Dr. Dermody prescribed ten days of Promethium. I had allergic reaction including hives. I took Provera for ten days this Spring but it did not induce the menstrual cycle. I recall you saying that it may need to take more to induce it due to the Tegretal. Please see letter from Dr. Dermody.

The Hologic Sahara Bone Sonometer scan of my left foot a few months ago recorded a negative 1.6, a moderate level for Osteoporosis. Dr.'s Dermody, Garcia, and Girgiss, all recommended 1500 mg. calcium

Three Year Check-Up continued

supplements, walking, as well as adding resistance and weight bearing exercises to build bones. Dr. Girgiss said there are better bone density scan tests available than the foot.

Thank you for all your help with these medical concerns, and for all that you have done to help me.

God bless you,

Carla

"A wise man will hear and increase in learning, And a man of understanding will acquire wise counsel.

> Proverbs 1:5

"This will bring healing to your body and refreshment to your bones."

> Proverbs 3:8

Turn the page for YOUR TURN

Your Turn

Are you partnering with medical doctors to monitor your health? Are you keeping them updated on your condition?

Your Turn

45 Finding Rest

Taking care of myself included rest and relaxation. Without sleep, my body couldn't function and I became susceptible to illness. Adequate sleep is recommended for anyone living with seizures and I was no exception.

Keeping a balance of work and play and rest needed to be a top priority for me. Lack of sleep left me prone to seizures. Lack of sleep left me feeling edgy, anxious, and wore out. To avoid fretting over what was not done; I remembered there is always tomorrow. I could ask for help, or I could say "no" to some things. Living in balance proved healthier than dealing with added stress.

To do my part to limit seizures, I had to have at least eight hours of sleep. If I was up late or out with friends till early morning hours, I needed to get a nap that next day. I didn't have seizures every time but I felt weak and sleepy. Foggy thinking increased my chances of having a seizure. When I was in the epilepsy evaluation center, they deprived me of sleep to induce seizures for the video taping and monitoring.

"The way of a fool is right in his own eyes, But a wise man is he who listens to counsel."

Proverbs 12:15

Your Turn

How can you simplify your life and alleviate extra things you don't need to be doing? Asking for help from others is okay.

Take time for yourself. Do one thing good for yourself today. Saying "no" to extra things is okay. Let go of unnecessary burdens.

Elevator Going Down
Emotions - Ground Floor

Eventually, my thoughts and feelings hit rock bottom. My lack of confidence and low self esteem created a barrier between what I felt inside and what I pretended to be on the outside. Outwardly, I appeared to be fine.

Internally, my body, soul, and inner thoughts were not at peace. I was tied in knots, bound up in a negative pattern of thinking. Meditating on the wrong things only caused me to feel weak, helpless, and burdened with fear, worry, and low self worth. Through many years of counseling and journaling, I learned to train my mind to think and speak words that built me up.

I let myself enjoy the life that God has for all of us. When I got a taste of this true feeling of peace, it was like having my hands and feet unchained.

"And do not be conformed to this world, but be transformed by the renewing of your mind, so that you may prove what the will of God is, that which is good and acceptable and perfect."

Philippians 4:7

Your Turn

What burdens and fears cause you to feel tight and tense? What can you do to change this? Will worrying about this help?

Doubt

Don't overanalyze or underestimate your abilities before trying. Doubt is something unsettled and uncertain in one's mind or thoughts.

Often my worries, uncertainty, or concerns about what people think played like a broken record over and over in my mind. When I had an idea and wanted to move ahead, these doubts kept me from pursuing my dreams. Surgery gave me my life back and allowed me to return to normal daily activities. I could dream again.

I was determined not to let another day go by with negative thoughts to hold me back from achieving my dreams. The lesson I learned was to keep going, dust off my knees, get up, and launch forward to the next step on this new journey that leads down the road of success.

"Let us not lose heart in doing good, for in due time we will reap if we do not grow weary.

Galatians 6:9

Your Turn

Peace of mind is worth striving for. When in doubt – toss it out. What doubts can you toss out toward your own peace of mind?

Obsessing

I was obsessing over feelings and thoughts, anxiety and insecurities. Emotional eating is not the answer. Why do I turn to food for comfort?

My weakness is allowing myself to ponder while I graze in the food pantry. Lack of self control is a weakness that I have. I realize I need to take authority over my emotions and not allow my flesh to control my thoughts and actions.

Searching in the all the wrong places like the food pantry only caused me to feel like I have the control of this in my emotions when really it is less in control. I know that God is in control over all these things I have been enduring. Why have I've been allowing my emotions to take control? From this point on, I am making a decision to take control over my feelings.

When I feel in control, I feel confident. The need to build up our resistance to temptation over weakness got my attention.

The times I found myself looking entirely in wrong places have only caused me to be more anxious, fearful, and uncertain. My spirit feels crushed, worried, and desperate. Strength comes by knowing that God will never leave me nor forsake me and that His unconditional love will guide me through.

"I can do all things through Christ who strengthens me."

Philippians 4:13 (NKJV)

Your Turn

Are you battling for self control?
1. Realize and admit you have a problem.
2. Seek help, counsel, and support from friends and support groups.

49 Depression

Like a mouse in a maze, my mind raced with thoughts of doubt, fear, frustration, impatience, and disappointments. I added kindling to my mental fire by rehearsing what happened to me in the past, and building defenses for future injustices. I felt like I was all alone. This mind game of negative thinking, an everlasting habit, needed to be changed

I learned my lessons the hard way. I discovered that what I focus on in my mind is what I sow and reap in my life. I had to change my thinking to keep my thoughts at peace before, during, and after these mental times of trouble and uncertainties.

"We are destroying speculations and every lofty thing raised up against the knowledge of God, and we are taking every thought captive tot he obedience of Christ."

2 Corinthians 10:5.

Your Turn

What patterns of thought lead you into depression? What will you do next time your mind starts down that familiar path?

Fight or Flight

All my life, I lived as if I were walking with bare feet on broken glass. There are countless moments of uncertainty when I felt afraid of what would happen next after the seizures.

My experience with fight or flight feelings started with a chill in the lower spine and a chill in the back of my head. Accompanying the chills, I felt nervous, anxious, and uncertain of what would happen next. Not knowing how to deal with my feelings caused me to have unnecessary problems in my body.

It was the same feeling others get at the top of a roller coaster headed down. There's the sudden tingle and quick rush through the tailbone, sending chills through the body in a split second of time. Those fight or flight sensations can be scary and at that second when it would happen, I automatically tried to breathe calmly while I braced myself against a seizure.

The most stressful feelings in my life have been about my epilepsy and health issues. Seizures, auras, what ifs, pondering the next step, all led to fear and anxiety.

Presently, when I remember the past, those memories trigger those same emotions. When the fight or flight feelings happen, they leave me wondering what might happen next. A counselor helped me identify the problems and deal with them when they occur.

My older brother told me, "Carla, it is only ten seconds out of a 24 hour day that this happened. Don't let those few seconds ruin the rest of your day. We all have funny feelings, quirks, and what ifs."

I am in complete control and aware of my surroundings during these moments. Therefore, how I choose to deal with it is what matters. God, help me draw strength from you. May Your love comfort me through these uneasy feelings, thoughts and emotions (Carla).

Your Turn

Slowly, take a deep breath. Exhale even slower. Journal your fight or flight feelings.

What were you thinking at that time to help you identify the problem?

FEAR
False Evidence Appearing Real

Almost every morning, fear daily gripped my mind for many years. As the sun began to shine through my bedroom window, I felt the chilling rush tremble through my body. Weighing the feelings, I wondered what would happen next. Needing to gain control over my thoughts and hold my mind from racing, what should I do? My body felt like a pin cushion with tingly toes and prickly fingers.

These were major, full blown panic attacks caused by my mind rehearsing an overload of worries and concerns.

How could I take control over my thoughts? Would I make it through this test of times? How could I cope with this? I tried an anti-depressant medicine prescribed by my doctor, and I felt mellow but not very functional at work or at home.

My hope renewed when my neighbor gave me these words: "Carla, fear stands for False Evidence Appearing Real."

Seeking hope, strength, and faith from God helped. He gave me help through counseling, Christian friends, and social gatherings. I carried this scripture in my purse so I would have it everyday. The paper wilted into pieces over the three years I tightly held onto it. One day, I met a friend who was where I had been three year ago. I passed it on to her as I now pass it to you.

"You will not afraid of the terror by night Or of the arrow that flies by day; Of the pestilence that stalks in darkness, Or of the destruction that lays waste at noon. A thousand may fall at your side And ten thousand at your right hand, But it shall not approach you."

Psalm 91:5-7.

Your Turn

How much does fear control your life?

Balance

I needed balance. Balance in thought, work, play, and daily activities. Prioritizing what was necessary and not necessary. Learning to say "no" to activities that are not important was a process for me. Keeping a balance in my everyday events such as family, and career needed to be a priority for my well-being. Out of balance caused turmoil in my emotions and added much stress. Stress made me vulnerable to seizures.

When things feel out of control, it helps to know that God is in the center of my problems every second of the day.

Daily heartfelt prayers carry my inner concerns to the Lord. The devil comes to steal, kill, and destroy. It is hope and love we all need when the world seems dark and dingy. Hope is in God, our Father and the Creator of heaven and earth.

"...I will be with you; I will not fail you or forsake you."

Joshua 1:5

Your Turn

Where do you need balance in your life? What can you do to meet that goal?

53 Four Years After Surgery

July 11, 2005, a summer day in the Midwest, four years, eight months and four days after brain surgery. A new sunrise brightened the sky as I awoke. Birds chirped, ducks landed on the lake where we camped for the week in celebration of Independence Day.

I celebrated my own independence. Two weeks earlier I began reducing Tegretal XR from my daily doses of seizure medicines. Part of me was excited about this but a small part had concerns about decreasing. I needed to work on getting past the doubts in the back of my mind.

I recall lying in bed, my stomach churning while I waited for any repercussions. My mind was a stronghold of constantly rehashed negative feelings. Meditating on the fear and what ifs held me back. I had to choose to take control of my thoughts and retrain them to think good things. I knew I was well. I had never lost consciousness. I knew what a seizure was and I knew what an aura was. I had been fine for four years. I was a success story. This was my true self talk. For the race I had yet to run, my faith and the scriptures gave me the hope I needed. I chose to let the peace of God rule in my heart.

"Be anxious for nothing, but in everything, by prayer and supplication, with thanksgiving let your requests be known to God. And the peace of God, which surpasses all comprehension, will guard your hearts and your minds in Christ Jesus."

Philippians 4: 6-7.

Your Turn

What are your thoughts and concerns? Start your day with a word of hope and encouragement to carry you through the rocky moments. If you have a medical concern, address it with a medical doctor.

Five Year Anniversary And Pursuing Dreams

My husband, daughter, and I camped at the family farm with my husband's sister and her family. It was the fifth anniversary after surgery. The wind blew hard against the camper and tornado warnings made it difficult to sleep. Awake and listening to the wind, I marveled that the final chapter of recovery and remission after surgery for seizures had arrived. I had not had any full blown seizures characterized by nausea, tingling, and unconsciousness. Those first years were an exciting, adventurous, and emotionally challenging test of times and faith.

The only residual symptom I experienced was a tingle in the lower spine, and a churning in my stomach. Nothing like an aura or onset of a seizure, there was only a lump in my throat that went away after a swallow.

Was it an aura? A pseudo aura? It was so easy for my mind to travel down that well-trod thought process on the eve of the five year mark. Why would my mind choose to ponder on the past when I knew I had already beaten the odds?

I decided to put the past behind me. To throw away the old book as my surgeon told me on my checkup. Start a new book.

It is a continuing process. I get further in the running of the race and then something trips me up. Yet, I keep putting my feet forward to put the past behind.

"He said to her, 'Daughter, your faith has healed you. Go in peace and be freed from your suffering.'"

Mark 5:34 (NIV 2011)

Your Turn

Does fear of recurrences haunt your thoughts?

55
Five Years
Seizure or Anxiety?

Half awake in bed, I pondered the day's schedule of events. When I felt the tingle of chills, I recalled what my clinical psychologist taught me about coping with these feelings. He said they were feelings of anxiousness similar to those felt by a soldier fighting in a war who had fight or flight chills before a major attack.

The feeling in my stomach was akin to what I felt if I ran a stop sign. But they no longer led to an aura or seizure. On a scale of 0-10, I rated the sensation as a one. It lasted no longer than five seconds.

I recorded my thoughts in a journal during the first year of recovery. My doctors suggested I get help for my emotions and feelings from a qualified clinical psychologist. I found a doctor at the nearby hospital in our area.

A strong faith and trust in God gave me the strength and endurance to get through those moments of doubt, worried that a seizure was next. Anytime I gave into my worries, fears like fiery darts peppered my emotions. Instead, I learned to hold fast to my victory through Christ who gave me victory.

"Forget the former things; do not dwell in the past."

Isaiah 43:18 (NIV 2011)

Your Turn

What areas are going well in your life?

56 Perfectly Fine

Five years and two months after my surgery for epilepsy, I returned to the Mayo Clinic in Rochester, Minnesota for a review and follow-up visit. I met with my doctor, nurse, and a doctor in training.

My doctor declared the surgery a success and diagnosed me as perfectly fine. As I was still decreasing the seizure medicine, he agreed that I could continue yearly follow-up visits. He expected a 95 to 100 percent recovery rate. Astonishingly, the doctor said the left side of my brain was bigger than the right side. Five years ago, the right side of my brain was pulling the left side along, compensating for the seizures that were weakening the left side of the brain. God's favor and grace were all over this appointment.

My nurse recognized me in the hall prior to my appointment. During a previous phone call, she told me she was originally from the rural area where I live. We talked about home and my recovery.

Having Dr. Cascino as my physician was a marvelous display of God's will and favor and His divine love for me. In my times of trouble, God helped me. In my darkest hours of seizures, and messed up medicines, God opened doors that ultimately led to the Mayo Clinic in October, 2000.

"Beloved I wish above all things that you may prosper and be in health, even as thy soul prospers."

III John :2

Your Turn

What progress are you experiencing in your life?

57 Annual Check-Ups

Every year I return to the Mayo Clinic for my check up. Every year, something miraculously happens.

On my fifth year visit, I met a lady who believes in the power of healing. I had her pray over me the night before my medical visit with my doctor.

Back home from the clinic, our Pastor mentioned how he loves to research, study, and memorize scripture. He said that the left side of his brain must be larger than the right. Just like my brain. Pastor spoke about worrying as a form of meditation. He recommended I exchange my anxious thoughts for meditating on Philippians 4:19.

I was consumed with doubts, disbelief, and uncertainty. Was the churning in my stomach, the lump in my throat, the tingling in my back anxiety or an aura? Luke 24: 38 asks, "Why are you troubled and why do doubts rise in your mind?" I was worried about having a setback. While a setback would have pulled me down emotionally, my constant watching for a setback was having the same results on my emotional state.

"You have more important things to focus on," my brother Craig reminded, "like your daughter and husband who need you."

Doubts, fears, what ifs and uncertainty can hold you back from achieving the big plans that you have dreamed of. So, when in doubt, toss it out.

"Do not let your heart be troubled; believe in God..."

John 14:1

Your Turn

When anxieties and worries consume your thoughts, how will you take every thought captive and focus on more important issues?

Six Year Set-Back

November 7, 2006. It's been six years since my life-changing surgery. It is hard to believe it has been that long already. In January, 2006, my doctor released me since I had been seizure free for five years. On September 3, I was finally off all the medicines. It had been a five year process of reducing medicines to see how successful the surgery had been.

I woke in the night on October 30, thinking that I needed to get up to go to the bathroom. Instead, I nestled back into the best sleep I'd had in a long time. But that morning I woke to a blasting headache, my tongue sore where I'd bit it, and a wet spot in my underwear.

My husband explained I'd had a seizure in the night. He described that I sat up in bed and then laid down, curled in a ball. I foamed at the mouth and clinched my teeth while he comforted me. Nine minutes was a long time.

I recalled feeling tense earlier that day and feeling the recourse of an aura the morning before. It was the first time since surgery I had experienced that sensation of an aura and related symptoms characteristic before a seizure. Like the nervous biting of my lower lip, or the drool, that happens after a seizure. These symptoms didn't reappear until I was completely off the medicine for 58 days though I could sense over the previous ten days that each day I was growing more tense.

I was starting the meds again on October 31, but the seizure occurred the night before. The nurse at Mayo Clinic advised I resume a daily dose of 200 mg. Tegretal. For the first time in six years, I wished that I was at the Mayo Clinic getting help from Dr. Cascino. With the initial dose of 100 mg. of Tegretal, I felt a loud sizzle in my temporal area like soda fizzing in my head. The splitting headaches dissipated. When the dose was increased to 400 mg. the hollow sound in the left side of my brain went away. The lower spine chills, and the stomach churning got better.

Six Year Set-Back continued

Occasionally I get a small tingle in my lower spine, leg, and thigh. It feels like a premonition that something is about to happen. I had a tremor in my hands on December 7, a slight drool, and a feeling like a hand was pressing on the back of my head.

I need to slow down and take time for quietness, solitude meditating and soul searching so I can see how big my God is, and how small my troubles really are.

"God is within her, she will not fall; God will help her at the break of day."

Psalm 46:5 (NIV 2011)

Turn the page for YOUR TURN

Your Turn

Have you experienced a major set back just when things were looking good?

Your Turn

59 Medicine Free

I was ready to let go of the apron strings that held me secure in my thoughts. With the approval of my neurologist, I stopped taking the 100 mg. of Tegretal I had relied on for five months. I was emotionally, mentally, physically, and most importantly medically, approved to do this before completely coming off the seizure medication.

Labor Day, September 3, 2006 found me camping with the family. I had taken the last seizure pill. I was medicine free for the first time in forty years. I needed to do this to see how successful the surgery had been before my six year checkup at the Mayo clinic.

The first thirty days felt like a let down. My nervous system was on edge. In the evening, as I lay down to sleep, my eyes would not close for long. They wanted to stay open. I tossed and turned in my sleep.

The second month off the meds was challenging. I developed feelings of withdrawal. My mind seemed separate from my body. My thoughts were short and edgy. My mom told me I didn't sound like myself. She said I talked slow and my voice dragged like I was sad. I noticed the impatience coupled with anger and my attention was very hard to maintain.

A red flag occurred on October 30th when I experienced that familiar nibble feeling in my lower lip that I used to get before a seizure. I had the blurred vision feeling like a panic attack. This caused me to pause and wait, aware of my response. There was no rushing in my stomach, no nauseousness, and no tingling in my head. But my body wanted to curl up as I was standing. I felt weak and my muscles ached as the days went by. But I had not lost consciousness.

Then, in the middle of the night I had a long, hard, nine minute seizure. According to my husband, my jaw clamped shut, and I rolled in a ball, and foamed at the mouth. I should have called the Mayo Clinic when I felt my first symptoms.

"I am exceedingly afflicted; revive me, O Lord, according to Your Word."

Psalm 119:107.

Your Turn

Have you ignored physical symptoms that were there to catch your attention? Is there something that is nagging to get your attention today?

First Reoccurring Seizure After Surgery

For five years and 51 weeks after surgery, I was seizure free. It was a marvelous milestone, the longest time in my life without seizures, auras, or medical setbacks. For two months after surgery, I was medicine free.

Then, while sleeping on October 30, 2006 I had a nine minute seizure. I had to return to taking the seizure medicines. My neurologist's nurse practitioner advised 200 mg. of Tegretal. When the strength of the auras increased, and I felt the familiar adrenalin rush of energy rage through my body, I called the Mayo Clinic for advice.

The Tegretal dose was doubled to 400 mg. the therapeutic level to control the seizures. Right away I noticed the difference the medicine made in my body. It takes some time to adjust but this proved to be the right amount to control the seizures from occurring.

It took a little time to readjust the right amount of medicines that I needed to best fit my medical needs.

Obviously being seizure free after surgery had been tremendously helpful to my mental and medical state of being.

"The troubles of my heart are enlarged; Bring me out of my distresses. Look upon my affliction and my trouble, And forgive all my sins."

Psalm 25:17-18

"Be not wise in your own eyes; Fear the Lord, and turn away from evil. It shall be healing to your body And refreshment to your bones."

Proverbs 3:7-8

Your Turn

How have your challenges affected other areas of your physical body?

61 Conflicting Symptoms

The first half of September, I felt no difference off the medicines except a let down feeling coming off the Tegretal. The third and forth week, I felt an extra boost of energy and clear vision. I had sensations in my skin, muscles, and nerves I had never felt before. I felt light as a feather, like I was floating.

But for the first half of October, my attention and my mind were difficult to keep focused. My emotional fuse shortened and I easily became angry or frustrated. My daughter commented on my impatience with her.

By the third week of October, it was harder to sleep at night. I tossed and turned. My arms felt weak. During the final weekend, 58 days without medications, the tenseness began to develop. That night, the seizure began at 4:00 a.m. and lasted nearly ten minutes.

It is not a failure: it is discovery.

"And without faith it is impossible to please God, because anyone who comes to him must believe that he exists and that he rewards those who earnestly seek him."

Hebrews 11:6 (NIV 2011)

Your Turn

Is someone noticing something that you should pay attention to?

62 Restarting Medicines

The doctor recommended a therapeutic dose of 400 mg. Tegretal to prevent further seizures. Now I felt more like myself, though the transition didn't come easy. I wrestled with stress surrounding personal and career issues, as well as the changing sensations of my body. Sometimes my blood felt hot. Sometimes it felt cold. As I increased the dosage, I had to adjust to differences in my vision, and an overall dopey feeling. Emotionally, I was disappointed that medicine was once again a major factor in my life.

I had my hormones tested to rule out imbalances. The ENT (ear, nose, and throat) doctor reviewed my sinuses and hearing. The ringing in my ears was from the medication.

To help alleviate anxiety, I opted for smaller meals and eliminated junk food. An improved diet and eating six small meals, which I still do, proved key to promoting balance.

"In this world you shall have trouble. But take heart! I have overcome the world."

John 16:33 (NIV 2011)

Your Turn

Are there changes you can make in your diet that will improve your health?

63 What If I Have A Seizure?

What I had most feared had happened. The "what if" had become reality. *What I fear comes upon me, and what I dread befalls me* (Job 3:25). The morning after the seizure occurred, I had to pry loose the anxiety that gripped my mind. My thoughts once more became a battle ground of what would have, could have, and should have happened. How would I overcome what happen?

It was my choice to decide if I would allow fear to occupy my mind.

What ifs pull me down. They add stress and anxiety, unnecessary burdens that can be a catalyst for many ailments including increased seizure activity.

Learning from past experiences, I found that thoughts are powerful to my body, mind, and emotional well being. I switched from being on guard for the next "what if" to beginning each day intently to live, give, and enjoy. Doubt was not my friend. I had to rise to a higher level that included loving me, caring for myself, and resting on the promise of my future in Christ Jesus.

I was surprised by the power of my thoughts over my actions. When I retrained my thoughts, my actions improved and those better actions became better habits. Improved habits affected my character and my character determines my destiny in life.

I have control over my destiny and I am worth every bit of effort to make it happen. God has a purpose and plan for me and for you. He says so in His word.

"For I know the plans I have for you, 'declares the Lord,' plans for welfare and not for calamity to give you a future and a hope.

Jeremiah 29:11

Your Turn

When you listen to your thoughts today, are they speaking of a promising future?

64 Adapting And Living With Epilepsy

Changes require adapting. Challenges may include limited driving ability and giving up some valued independence. I know first hand the trial of facing setbacks. Here is what I had learned to help me live well with a chronic condition.

Know what you need to know and what to expect.

Research. Ask questions. Be a sleuth and investigate everything you can about your conditions, and treatment options.

Be proactive in your treatment.

Make decisions that are important for you, your health, and well being.

Stay active and lead a full life.

Exercise, eat right, and maintain a positive outlook. Keep pursuing your dreams. Plan to succeed and work your plan.

Set goals.

Set reasonable goals that you can achieve. Never give up on the dreams. Focus on solutions.

Keep a strong, moral support group.

Develop a bond with others who have experienced similar circumstances. Keep ongoing contact. Join a local support group or start a group of your own.

Keep faith and hope alive in your spirit.

When setbacks rear their ugly heads, remind yourself that you made it through difficult times in the past. Friends will prove to be angels carrying you through hard times. Talk over your concerns with others. Never give up. Certainly you have a condition, but the condition does not have you. Spread your wings and soar like a butterfly.

When we say something is impossible, God says all things are possible (Luke 18:27).

Adapting And Living continued

When we think we can't go on, God promises that His grace is sufficient (II Corinthians 12:9).

When we feel we can't manage, God assures He will supply all our needs (Philippians 4:19).

When we are afraid, God gives us a spirit of power, love, and a sound mind (II Timothy 1:7).

When we wonder if we're alone, God reminds us that He will never leave or forsake us (Hebrews 13:5).

God is bigger than my problem.

Turn the page for YOUR TURN.

Your Turn

What goals and dreams do you want to set and achieve? What ten things can you do to start stepping towards the goals you want to see happen in your life? What is your time frame for these goals and dreams to be met? Speak in faith to your circumstances and claim your dream, and see yourself doing these desires and dreams. You can do it!

Your Turn

65 Adjusting To Changes

They say change is good. I agree as long as there is good to come from it. It's the adjusting to the changes that was hard for me. My tolerance for pain and my tolerance for sensory change were slim to none. It helped to have a great support team to guide me through.

I talked to a friend who experienced some of the same symptoms with Tegretal. She assured me that these were expected side affects.

The support of medical advice came in handy when we considered increasing the dose to ease the uncertain feelings I was having. But the extra medication caused me to feel buzzy. I'm thankful for the nurse at my doctor's office who walked me through that difficult day. The side affects from, medicines can play havoc on a body at times when adjusting, adding or decreasing medicines. Dizziness, fuzziness, vertigo feelings, and tolerating adjustments to the medicines physically and psychologically can be trying at times. Slow adjustments are the best and following my doctor's advice and directions are what I have and will to continue to follow.

It was a process, but I have adjusted to the changes. I feel better. Adjusting to the change and adjusting to medicines can both be very trying.

"Do not fear, for I am with you; Do not anxiously look about you, for I am your God I will strengthen you, surely I will help you, Surely I will uphold you with My righteous right hand."

Isaiah 41:10

Your Turn

What adjustments have you had to make in your medications or lifestyle that unwelcome at first proved beneficial?

Denial

"It's not true! It was just a bad dream. I couldn't have had a seizure."

"I don't need the support. I'll be okay. I can do this myself."

How many times had those thoughts crossed my mind? Who was I kidding except myself? Who was I hurting except myself? The truth was that to take control of my health and well being, I did need my family and the help of others.

Everybody needs somebody. I could choose to accept care for myself. I could not, and still cannot, get through this alone. Moving past the denial stage was the first step in the right direction.

I needed professional wisdom and advice from a specialized medical team of neurologists, physicians, support groups, and counselors.

I began to accept the fact that it was okay to be in denial, but not okay to stay there. The next step was to stop wasting time worrying over what should have, would have, or could have been different had I done this or that. I made the decision to forget former things and to stop dwelling on the past. I had to retrain my thoughts to focus on the good in my life. To think on what I could do rather than what I could not do. Maybe I couldn't do everything but I could do something. Who can I help? Where can I make a difference?

"Then he said to Thomas, 'Put your finger here; see my hands. Reach out your hand and put it into my side. Stop doubting and believe."

John 20:27

Your Turn

What are the words of denial that are common in your thought life? What words will you replace them with?

Rejection

The more time goes by, the more distant something becomes in my thoughts. That's what my counselor, Dr. Abramson told me. After 2,482 days without a seizure or setback following surgery, I had become less on guard. How good it felt to relax.

The night after the seizure, fear and worry once again consumed my mind. The negative thinking that had become distant, now dominated my thoughts.

My body responded by building a defense. Fight or flight feelings coursed through my veins. I noticed chills, tingles, and a reluctance to release control and go to sleep.

The new challenge was to take responsibility for my mental attitude. I had to first accept these understandable emotions, and move past them in a positive direction. This was necessary for my well-being and for the well-being of my family.

I did this by seeking professional counseling and medical support. I released my emotions and thoughts into a journal. I surrounded myself with positive people and faced one day at a time.

It is regimen that my body needs to function properly.

"And we know that in all things God works for the good of those who love him, who have been called according to his purpose"

Romans 8:28.

Your Turn

What is your response to setbacks?

Acceptance

Today I accept the fact that I need to take medication to control seizures. I accept the fact that the surgery was a huge success. I accept the fact that I made the long journey from surgery to reducing the medications until I was medicine free. I accept the fact that I learned a lot about my body including the proper balance of medication, rest, nutrition, and worry less; that now allows me to live my life without seizures.

In six years, I came a long way.

The morning after the seizure, the nurse asked, "How much stress were you under?"

"A lot."

Restarting the medication was like connecting two puzzle pieces together. My mind, emotions, and nerves felt complete.

To aid the process, I began to quote with a friend ten blessings for which I am thankful. Laughing and doing fun things with others became a priority. Deciding to give my best, to live with purpose, and to help others in return helped me.

I cannot change the past. I cannot reverse what has been done. I can make the choice to accept the responsibility to get past the areas that try to hold me back. Acceptance is the turning point to moving ahead. Never have regrets!

Serenity Prayer

God grant me the serenity to accept the things I cannot change; courage to change the things I can; and wisdom to know the difference.

Your Turn

What ten blessings are you thankful for?

Moving Ahead

69

I've left behind the former things that tried to hold me back, and hamper my dreams. My course is set, full speed ahead. My focus is to do the best I can in what I can do.

Paul described running the race that lies ahead to finish well. He admonished us to put the past behind and press on toward the victory. In those stormy times, I have felt like there was no end to the strong winds that tossed me like a cork in a rough sea. Paul literally felt that way when the ship he traveled on was trapped for days in a dangerous storm.

I felt tossed in an emotional and physical storm. I'm thankful the worst is behind me. Now I can make more progressive progress toward my goals. Run the race and press on towards the victory.

"Not that I have already obtained all this, or have already arrived at my goal, but I press on to take hold of that for which Christ Jesus took hold of me. Brothers and sisters, I do not consider myself yet to have taken hold of it. But one thing I do: Forgetting what is behind and straining toward what is ahead, I press on toward the goal to win the prize for which God has called me heavenward in Christ Jesus."

Philippians 3:12-14.

Your Turn

What dream are you pressing forward to today?

Victory Lane

A 95 to 100 percent success rate is the outcome I was looking for when I chose to have brain surgery. Every November 7th, I marked the anniversary of that major event in my life. Every year that goes by seizure free is a major achievement, a celebrated milestone.

On a daily basis, some days were awesome, some were average, and some were plagued with anxiety, stress, negative thoughts, and self doubts.

Physically, the surgery paved the way for miraculous freedom and a better life style. As difficult as it was to recover from brain surgery and wean off a lifetime of medications, the more challenging task was training my thoughts and emotions to take a different track. When I turned my focus away from negative expectations, and focused on a more free future, that was when I found myself traveling down victory lane.

"Consider it pure joy, my brothers, whenever you face trials of many kinds because you know that the testing of your faith produces perseverance. Let perseverance finish its work so that you may be mature and complete, not lacking anything."

James 1:2 – 4

Your Turn

What emotional and mental changes are you making?

Living Life To The Fullest

My dream is to give hope. To all people who travel a hard road, whether it be mentally, physically, financially, or emotionally, I want to walk alongside and assure them that there is a bright tomorrow. The darkest day does not last forever, though it feels like it surely will.

I had never dreamed big, thought big, or pursued big ideas until after having surgery for seizures. Nothing is too big or too small for you and me to achieve.

Never stop pursuing your dreams.

"For I am confident of this very thing, that He who began a good work in you will perfect it until the day of Christ Jesus."

Philippians 1:6.

Your Turn

What are your dreams? How will you get there?

72 Pursuing Dreams

Putting the past behind and not digging up the old dirt is hard to do. Burdens of guilt over past heartbreaks weighed me down.

Releasing past frustrations and failures felt good inside. Love is the greatest commandment of all and the most pleasing to the loving Father in heaven. I made a conscious effort to do right with neighbors, family members, co-workers, and strangers. The greatest feeling was forgiving the ones who hurt me in the past.

Life is too short to waste the precious time we have here on earth. I wanted to make a positive difference in the world around me. Helping others helped me find joy and happiness.

I had to take a hard look at why I held on to past hurts. It required that I dig deep to the root of the matter deep within my heart. The next step was to deal with my hurts, and the emotional thoughts that played in my mind.

"This I command you, that you love one another."

John 15: 17

Your Turn

Is there someone you need to forgive?

73 Inner Growth

The words I speak to myself and how I speak to others can either build up people or tear them down. Being sensitive to who I hang around with and how they talk around me and others either builds me up or tears me down. Growth of my inner being is a foundation of self worth and determines how I value myself. How I value myself can determine my destiny, future, and character. Choosing friends whose words are harsh, cold, and demeaning tears my self confidence. The world is filled with wonderful opportunities that God desires for His peoples to take hold of.

Not one of us is perfect, but I can make a difference in somebody's life by choosing to help others. Helping others helps me when I shift my energy from myself to others. It diverts my attention from me and onto others who need it. Lifting someone's spirit lifts my spirit as well.

"Therefore, do not throw away your confidence, which has a great reward."

Hebrews 10:35

Your Turn

Who can you help today? What can you do to help someone have a better life?

74 Setting The Stage

My past does not define my future. I do. It is important to see the big picture for my future. Maybe the things of the past did not go the way I planned it to go. Others who read this will understand the rehearsing that can go on in the mind can only be a mental drain and physical strain. Things are not always what they seem. Setting the stage is like the light bulb turned on brightly to a new day and new beginnings. Not allowing the past to define me, but to begin every day for success and expecting great things to happen.

Everything that has happened up until now is setting the stage for blessings and breakthroughs that are about to unfold. Set the stage with the image of being more than conquerors. He is able to do far more than we can ever imagine. Set your eyes on the size of how big our God is.

It is time to see the dreams and hopes in your life unfold before your eyes. He puts people in our lives so that we can find support from others during difficult times.

Fellowship is a gift from God.

"Now to him who is able to do far more abundantly beyond all that we ask or think, according to the power that works within us."

Ephesians 3:20

Your Turn

Think about this. When we make mistakes, something good comes from it. You mean the world to someone. Remember the compliments you have received from others. What are some of the words of encouragements you have been told by others? Hold onto your faith and let the healing take place! What miracles are you hoping for? Write them down in this journal of hope for God is able to do far more than ever imagined!

75 Unburdening Baggage

I took a deep breath, relaxed, and imagined a picture of the heavy baggage that weighed me down mentally and physically. I pictured the burden being tossed onto God's lap and at His feet. I visualized His arms extended out to me.

He has the same offer for everyone. Whether the problem is small or enormous. No matter what the topic. Throwing it all over to Jesus as He lifted those burdens and weights off my shoulders, I got a glimpse of His hands and arms waiting patiently to calm my worries. This vision of His warmth soothed me. In His word, God invites each of us to cast all cares upon the Lord. In peace I could lie down and sleep.

Why did I feel anxious and burdened, always rushing around? It was hard to change core habits. I listened to how my body felt, emotionally and spiritually, wanting to get to the heart of the matter and deal with these issues in my life.

I asked God for wisdom. He showed me that selfishness, pride, envy, and boasting were heavy burdens that had to be taken to the cross and dealt with by forgiving and speaking it outwardly. Past hurts from childhood had taken a hold on me. I had to purge bitterness, rage and anger, brawling and slander, along with every form of malice (Ephesians 4:31).

God reminded me that I need not worry about tomorrow. Today has enough worries in itself (Matt 6:34). I wanted to reach that point where I could lay my head down and sleep the whole night without any interruptions. This required effort, faith, hope, trust, and surrender of the flesh. I believe all things are possible to those who believe.

Just like my bed is in the same spot when I lie down and when I wake up, God sent His son Jesus to never leave me nor forsake me. In any time of need, the Lord is trustworthy to all who come to Him.

> "Come to me all you who are weary and heavy-laden, and I will give you rest."
>
> Matthew 11:28

Your Turn

Let's walk the faith journey together. It begins with making that decision to change. Next, we take baby steps to the finish line of victory. Jesus is the same yesterday, today, and tomorrow. Just like the rainbow that God sent as a symbol of His promise to never flood the earth again, He promises to finish what He began in you and me. What baby step will you take today to apply into your life?

From The Living Hope

Dear Friend,

I pray that you may enjoy good health and that all will go well with you, even as your soul is getting along well.

3 John 1: 2 (NIV 2011)

I Am

From Me To You

Dear Friend,
    May your life be filled with much hope, love, joy, peace, prosperity, bright tomorrows and a promising future!
There Is Hope!

Carla

RESOURCES FOR NEUROLOGICAL DISORDERS

Epilepsy Foundation: (1-800-332-1000) www.epilepsyfoundation.org
National Association of Epilepsy Centers: www.naecepilepsy.org
Citizens United for Research in Epilepsy (CURE) www.CUREepilepsy.org (1 312-255-1801)
Surge-Weber Foundation (1-800-627-5482) www.sturge-weber.com
Helping Paws (seizure dogs): (1-800-771-7221) www.canineassistants.org
Delta Society: www.deltasociety.org
National Institute of Neurological Disorders and Stroke: www.ninds.nih.gov
"The Brain Matters" (AAN Foundation patient's website): www.neurofoundation.org
Alzheimer's Association: (1-800-272-3900) www.alz.org
Autism Society of America (1-800-328-8476) www.autism-society.org
ALS Association (1-800-782-4747) www.alsa.org
Depression and Bipolar Support Alliance: (1-800-826-3632) www.dbsalliance.org
National Alliance for the Mentally Ill: (1-800-950-6264) www.nami.org
National Institute of Mental Health: (1-866-615-6464) www.nimh.nih.gov
Michael J. Fox Foundation for Parkinson Research: (1-800-708-7644) www.michaeljfox.org
National Headache Foundation: (1-888-643-5552) www.headaches.org
Muscular Dystrophy Association: (1-800-344-4863) www.mda.org
Multiple Sclerosis Foundation: (1-800-225-6495) www.msfocus.org
American Pain Foundation: (1-888-615-7246) www.painfoundation.org
American Stroke Association: (1-888-478-7653) www.strokeassociation.org
Trauma: Brain Injury Association of America: (1-800-444-6443) www.biausa.org
Brain Trauma Foundation (1-212-772-0608) www.braintrauma.org
National Spinal Cord Injury Association: (1-800-962-9629) www.spinalcord.org

Source: *Neurology Now*, page 47, July/August 2006 ;
Neurology Now, page 36-38, January/February 2009

Author's Contact Information

Carla Huelsmann
P.O. Box 115
Trenton, IL 62293

Office: 618.224.9736
Cell: 618.910.7832

email: carlahuelsmann@sbcglobal.net

CPSIA information can be obtained at www.ICGtesting.com
Printed in the USA
LVOW07s0512120914

403763LV00001B/4/P